Easy Wok Cookbook

Learn Over 77 Recipes For Preparing at Home Delicious Asian Stir Fried Dishes

---

Adele Tyler

© **Copyright 2021 by Adele Tyler - All rights reserved.**

This document is geared towards providing exact and reliable information in regard to the topic and issue covered. The publication is sold with the idea that the publisher is not required to render accounting, officially permitted, or otherwise, qualified services. If advice is necessary, legal or professional, a practiced individual in the profession should be ordered.

From a Declaration of Principles which was accepted and approved equally by a Committee of the American Bar Association and a Committee of Publishers and Associations.

In no way is it legal to reproduce, duplicate, or transmit any part of this document in either electronic means or printed format. Recording of this publication is strictly prohibited and any storage of this document is not allowed unless with written permission from the publisher. All rights reserved.

The information provided herein is stated to be truthful and consistent, in that any liability, in terms of inattention or otherwise, by any usage or abuse of any policies, processes, or directions contained within is the solitary and utter responsibility of the recipient reader. Under no circumstances will any legal responsibility or blame be held against the publisher for any reparation, damages, or monetary loss due to the information herein, either directly or indirectly.

Respective authors own all copyrights not held by the publisher.

The information herein is offered for informational purposes solely and is universal as so. The presentation of the information is without contract or any type of guarantee assurance.

The trademarks that are used are without any consent, and the publication of the trademark is without permission or backing by the trademark owner. All trademarks and brands within this book are for clarifying purposes only and are owned by the owners themselves, not affiliated with this document.

Contents

INTRODUCTION **9**

CHAPTER 1: WELCOME TO THE WORLD OF WOK BREAKFAST RECIPES **10**

1.1 Wok Chicken Omelettes 10

1.2 Wok Shashuka 11

1.3 Wok Seared Mushroom Omelettes 13

1.4 Wok Crispy Lemon Breakfast Potatoes 14

1.5 Wok Eggs and Tomatoes 15

1.6 Wok Breakfast Fried Rice 16

1.7 Wok Sausage Breakfast Skillet 17

1.8 Wok Breakfast Brown Rice 18

1.9 Wok Fried Eggs with Chili Sauce 20

1.10 Wok Crispy Hash Browns 21

1.11 Wok Breakfast Quinoa and Wild Rice 23

1.12 Wok Eggs and Carrot Stir Fry 24

1.13 Wok scrambled Egg with Prawns 25

1.14 Wok Beef and Broccoli Omelette 27

1.15 Wok Ham and Egg Fried Rice 28

1.16 Wok Ground Lamb and Eggs 29

CHAPTER 2: THE WORLD OF WOK LUNCH RECIPES 31

2.1 Wok Firecracker Chicken 31

2.2 Wok Chicken Chowmein 32

2.3 Wok Cabbage Stir-Fry 33

2.4 Wok Beef Pho 34

2.5 Wok Seared Salmon 36

2.6 Wok Fried Shrimp with Garlic 37

2.7 Wok Fried Malaysian Noodles 38

2.8 Wok Fried Macaroni 39

2.9 Wok Peanuts and Chicken 41

2.10 Wok Smoked Salmon 42

2.11 Wok Broccoli with Oyster Sauce 43

2.12 Wok Mongolian Chicken 44

2.13 Wok Almond Vegetable Stir Fry 45

2.14 Wok Sweet and Sour Beef 46

2.15 Wok Turkey Asparagus Stir-Fry 48

2.16 Wok Snappy Chicken Stir -Fry 50

CHAPTER 3: THE WORLD OF WOK DINNER RECIPES 51

3.1 Wok Coconut Shrimp Curry 51

3.2 Wok Mandarin Pork Stir-Fry 52

3.3 Wok Asparagus Tofu Stir-Fry 54

3.4 Wok Balsamic Pork Stir-Fry 55

3.5 Wok Beef Orange Stir-Fry.. 56

3.6 Wok Sizzling Chicken Lo Mein 58

3.7 Wok Chicken Soba Noodle Toss... 59

3.8 Wok Peking Shrimp 61

3.9 Wok Curried Fried Rice with Pineapple 62

3.10 Wok Ginger Peach Pork.. 63

3.11 Wok Nutty Chicken Fried Rice 65

3.12 Wok Honey Garlic Chicken Stir-Fry................................. 66

3.13 Wok Chicken Teriyaki... 67

3.14 Wok Honey Soy Wings.. 69

3.15 Wok Lime and Chili Chicken 70

3.16 Wok Potato and Chicken Stir-Fry 71

CHAPTER 4: THE WORLD OF WOK SNACK RECIPES
.... 73

4.1 Wok Fried Prawn Crackers 73

4.2 Wok Popcorn 74

4.3 Wok Egg Rolls... 75

4.4 Wok Chili Bamboo Shoots 77

4.5 Wok Scallion Pancakes 78

4.6 Wok Stuffed Mushrooms 79

4.7 Wok Zucchini Pancakes 80

4.8 Wok Avocado Egg Rolls.. 82

6

4.9 Wok Sticky Rice Dumplings 84

4.10 Wok Pork and Fish Dumplings 85

4.11 Wok Cream Cheese Wontons 86

4.12 Wok Sesame Pancakes 87

4.13 Wok Kimchi Pancakes 89

4.14 Wok Carrot Pancakes 90

CHAPTER 5: THE WORLD OF WOK VEGETARIAN RECIPES 92

5.1 Wok Seared Tofu 92

5.2 Wok Vegan Yaki Udon 93

5.3 Wok Vegan Kimchi Fried Rice 94

5.4 Wok Fried Greens 96

5.5 Wok Kale Mushroom and Cashew Stir-Fry 97

5.6 Wok Seared Vegetables 98

5.7 Wok Vegan Japchae 99

5.8 Creamy Coconut Vegetarian Wok 100

5.9 Stir-fried Cucumber 102

5.10 Teriyaki Vegetable Stir-Fry 103

5.11 Carrot Stir-Fry 105

5.12 Vegan Stir Fry with Tempeh and Rice 106

5.13 Sesame Ginger and Tofu Stir-Fry 107

5.14 Pumpkin Stir-Fry 108

5.15 Wok Vegetable Chowmein 110

CONCLUSION..**112**

Introduction

The word wok really signifies the cooking pot in Cantonese, so its motivation is completely clear. In any case, these early models were ordinarily made of solid metal material, which upgraded the wok's toughness. Archeologists have also discovered little, adjusted bits of earthenware in antiquated Chinese burial chambers demonstrating its ubiquity as far back as 200 BC.

In any case, history specialists are uncertain about the wok's precise inceptions. Evidently, the Chinese did not actually think often about licenses. They had a propensity for acquiring innovations from close by societies, including those from India, Thailand and different zones in the Southeast and across the more noteworthy mainland.

Stir-frying is a quick and better approach to cook. Basically it is the mixing of reduced down bits of food in a little hot oil in a wok over high warmth. Vegetables are made fresh and brilliant. Meats are tasty, delicate, and very much crispy. Stir-frying turned into an essential Chinese cooking strategy during the Ming Dynasty and at last, the method advanced toward America with Chinese migrants. It is amusing to blend and match fixings when sautéing.

Chapter 1: Welcome to the World of Wok Breakfast Recipes

A wok distributes heat equally from the base and up the sides, and on account of the precarious sides; you can move food around in it. This part contains sound and simple to make breakfast plans.

1.1 Wok Chicken Omelettes

Preparation time: 15 minutes
Cooking Time: 10 minutes
Serving: 2

Ingredients:
- Green onions, two
- Sesame oil, two tsp.
- Fried shallots, two tbsp.
- Beans sprouts, half cup
- Sweet chili sauce, one tbsp.
- Soy sauce, two tbsp.
- Peanut oil, two tbsp.
- Salt to taste
- Black pepper to taste
- Chicken, two cups
- Eggs, four

Instructions:

1. In a small container, whisk together all fixings well.
2. Whisk eggs, onion and one tablespoon water in a medium bowl.
3. Warm a wok over high warmth.
4. Add a large portion of the sesame oil and a large portion of the nut oil to wok; whirl to cover surface.
5. Pour into equal parts the egg blend and whirl to shape an omelet.
6. Top with a large portion of the chicken, and other toppings.
7. Sprinkle omelets with dressing.
8. Serve with shallots and coriander.

1.2 Wok Shashuka

Preparation time: 30 minutes

Cooking Time: 20 minutes

Serving: 6

Ingredients:

- Cheddar cheese, one cup
- Bacon, half cup
- Green onions, three tbsp.
- Bell pepper strips, half cup

- Zucchini, two cups
- Chopped fresh dill, two tbsp.
- Vegetable oil, two tbsp.
- Soy sauce, two tbsp.
- Salt to taste
- Black pepper to taste
- Tomatoes, two cups
- Eggs, six
- Chopped onions, two tbsp.

Instructions:

1. Sauté the bacon in a wok until it starts to turn brown.
2. Add the onions and ringer peppers and cook, blending every now and again, until relaxed and delicately seared.
3. Mix in the tomatoes, at that point add the potatoes, and season with salt.
4. Add the beer and cook the potatoes until delicate.
5. Break the eggs, separating them over the potato, bacon and tomato combination.
6. Sprinkle over the cheddar.
7. Your dish is ready to be served.

1.3 Wok Seared Mushroom Omelettes

Preparation time: 15 minutes
Cooking Time: 30 minutes
Serving: 4

Ingredients:
- Fish sauce, two tbsp.
- Chopped garlic, two tsp.
- Green onions, three tbsp.
- Bell pepper strips, half cup
- Bean sprouts, one cup
- Chopped fresh dill, two tbsp.
- Vegetable oil, two tbsp.
- Soy sauce, two tbsp.
- Salt to taste
- Black pepper to taste
- Mushrooms, one cup
- Eggs, twelve

Instructions:
1. Join all the fixings in little bowl.
2. Join eggs and sauces in medium bowl; beat delicately.
3. Add a large portion of the vegetable combination to egg blend.
4. Warm a fourth of the vegetable oil in wok.

5. At the point when oil is simply smoking, add a fourth of the egg combination.
6. At the point when omelet is practically set, sprinkle a fourth of the leftover vegetables more than one portion of the omelet.
7. Cook briefly, turning the omelet fifty-fifty.
8. Serve your dish with different sauces.

1.4 Wok Crispy Lemon Breakfast Potatoes

Preparation time: 25 minutes

Cooking Time: 20 minutes

Serving: 2

Ingredients:
- Chopped bell pepper, one
- Green onions, three tbsp.
- Scallions, half cup
- Potatoes, two
- Chopped onions, one
- Lemon juice, two tbsp.
- Canola oil, two tbsp.
- Salt to taste
- Black pepper to taste

Instructions:

1. Add potatoes and oil to a wok.
2. Mix until the potatoes are all around covered with oil.
3. Spot the wok over medium-high warmth.
4. Cook until sautéed and delicate.
5. Add the rest of the ingredients to the wok.
6. Cook until the peppers and onions are delicate.
7. Mix in lemon juice and scallions.
8. Your dish is ready to be served.

1.5 Wok Eggs and Tomatoes

Preparation time: 5 minutes
Cooking Time: 5 minutes
Serving: 2

Ingredients:
- Sugar, a pinch
- Water, two tsp.
- Spring onions, three tbsp.
- Tomatoes, half cup
- Vegetable oil, two tbsp.
- Salt to taste
- Black pepper to taste
- Eggs, four

Instructions:

1. Strip off the peel of the tomatoes.
2. Beat the eggs with water.
3. Warm oil in a wok on high warmth.
4. Pour in eggs.
5. Take the egg out when there is not any more fluid.
6. Put one teaspoon of oil to a similar wok.
7. Cook garlic and tomatoes on medium warmth.
8. Mix in the eggs mixture.
9. Top with spring onion prior to serving.

1.6 Wok Breakfast Fried Rice

Preparation time: 10 minutes
Cooking Time: 10 minutes
Serving: 4

Ingredients:
- Soy sauce, two tbsp.
- Chopped garlic, two tsp.
- Green onions, three tbsp.
- Bacon strips, half cup
- Vegetable oil, two tbsp.
- Salt to taste
- Black pepper to taste
- Cooked rice, two cups
- Eggs, four

Instructions:
1. Warm a wok.
2. Add about a tablespoon of oil.
3. Add the eggs.
4. Add the diced or cut bacon and mix attempt until daintily cooked.
5. Add the ginger and garlic to the bacon.
6. Add your rice, somewhat more oil in the event that you need it and mix.
7. Add about a teaspoon of soy sauce and return the eggs to the wok.
8. Plate and serve quickly with more soy sauce.

1.7 Wok Sausage Breakfast Skillet

Preparation time: 10 minutes

Cooking Time: 20 minutes

Serving: 6

Ingredients:
- Chopped garlic, two tsp.
- Onions, three tbsp.
- Shredded cheddar cheese, half cup
- Potatoes, two
- Vegetable oil, two tbsp.

- Soy sauce, two tbsp.
- Salt to taste
- Black pepper to taste
- Water, half cup
- Eggs, six

Instructions:

1. In a wok, cook the sausage until cooked through.
2. Add garlic, diced potatoes, and water.
3. Add the onion.
4. Add a shower of oil if potatoes begin adhering to the lower part of the dish.
5. Add sausage back to the container.
6. Break eggs into the dish over high warmth and sprinkle destroyed cheddar onto the potatoes in the wok.
7. Let the edges of the eggs set.
8. Your dish is fit to be served.

1.8 Wok Breakfast Brown Rice

Preparation time: 25 minutes

Cooking Time: 10 minutes

Serving: 2

Ingredients:

- Hot sauce, two tbsp.

- Chopped garlic, two tsp.
- Green onions, three tbsp.
- Bacon strips, half cup
- Cooked brown rice, two cups
- Chopped fresh chives, two tbsp.
- Vegetable oil, two tbsp.
- Soy sauce, two tbsp.
- Salt to taste
- Black pepper to taste
- Avocado slices, as required
- Eggs, two
- Sesame oil, two tbsp.

Instructions:
1. Warm a wok over low warmth and add the bacon strips.
2. Include the eggs and mix continually with a wooden spoon until the eggs are simply mixed.
3. Pour the excess bacon fat in the wok.
4. Include the rice, at that point let it sit for two minutes to heat up and get crispy.
5. Mix, splitting up any pieces, and mix for an additional couple of moments.
6. Now, taste the rice and mix in the soy sauce.
7. Add the bacon and eggs back in to the wok and throw in the green onions.
8. Mix well and let sit over low warmth while you cook the eggs for garnish.

9. Cook eggs as wanted and season them with an intense of salt, pepper and squashed red pepper.
10. Add the egg on top alongside the avocado.
11. Your dish is fit to be served.

1.9 Wok Fried Eggs with Chili Sauce

Preparation time: 20 minutes
Cooking Time: 5 minutes
Serving: 2

Ingredients:
- Asian Sesame oil, two tbsp.
- Tomato, one
- Green onions, three tbsp.
- Soy sauce, half cup
- Chili sauce, one tbsp.
- Chopped fresh coriander, two tbsp.
- Peanut oil, two tbsp.
- Salt to taste
- Black pepper to taste
- Eggs, six

Instructions:

1. Cut the tomato down the middle and cut it into fine pieces.
2. Delicately beat the eggs in a bowl with the sesame oil, a large portion of the spring onion, and some salt and pepper to consolidate.
3. Blend the sauces.
4. Warm a wok over high warmth until hot; at that point add the nut oil.
5. Cook the egg combination until it is firm.
6. Disperse with the excess spring onion and the coriander twigs. At that point spoon over a portion of the readied sauce.
7. Your dish is fit to be served.

1.10 Wok Crispy Hash Browns

Preparation time: 15 minutes

Cooking Time: 15 minutes

Serving: 4

Ingredients:

- Vegetable oil, two tbsp.
- Soy sauce, two tbsp.
- Salt to taste
- Black pepper to taste
- Potatoes, two cups

Instructions:
1. Strip the potatoes.
2. Utilize an enormous holed cheddar grater or food processor to shred the potatoes.
3. Spot the potatoes in a colander and wash well, or until the water runs clear.
4. Just barely get the potatoes of their abundance water by squeezing against the side of the colander or crushing in your clench hand.
5. Warm an enormous cast iron or non-stick wok over medium warmth.
6. When hot, add a tablespoon of cooking oil.
7. Add a portion of the potatoes or enough to cover the outside of the wok in a strong, yet flimsy layer.
8. Allow the potatoes to broil, without upsetting, until profoundly brilliant earthy color appears on the base.
9. Flip the potatoes, and sprinkle with extra oil if necessary.
10. Allow the potatoes to cook on the second side without upsetting until brilliant earthy colored and firm once more.
11. Season softly on the subsequent side.
12. If necessary, flip and cook once again to accomplish the proportion of earthy colored to white that you like.
13. Your dish is fit to be served.

1.11 Wok Breakfast Quinoa and Wild Rice

Preparation time: 5 minutes
Cooking Time: 15 minutes
Serving: 4

Ingredients:

- Asian Sesame oil, one tbsp.
- Chopped garlic, two tsp.
- Green onions, three tbsp.
- Peas, half cup
- Carrots, two cups
- Butter, two tbsp.
- Oyster sauce, two tbsp.
- Soy sauce, two tbsp.
- Salt to taste
- Black pepper to taste
- Quinoa, two cups
- Eggs, two
- Chopped onions, two tbsp.
- White onion, one

Instructions:

1. Warm the butter in a huge wok over medium-high warmth until dissolved.
2. Add eggs, and cook until mixed.

3. Eliminate eggs.
4. Add the butter to the dish and warm it until dissolved.
5. Add the vegetables, and season with a liberal amount of salt and pepper.
6. Quickly add the rest of the ingredients including the sauces as well, and mix until joined.
7. Keep blending to sear the quinoa.
8. At that point include the eggs and mix to join.
9. Add the sesame oil.
10. Your dish is ready to be served.

1.12 Wok Eggs and Carrot Stir Fry

Preparation time: 5 minutes

Cooking Time: 5 minutes

Serving: 2

Ingredients:
- Sugar, a pinch
- Water, two tsp.
- Spring onions, three tbsp.
- Carrots, half cup
- Vegetable oil, two tbsp.
- Salt to taste
- Black pepper to taste
- Eggs, four

Instructions:
1. Strip off the peel of the carrots.
2. Beat the eggs with water.
3. Warm oil in a wok on high warmth.
4. Pour in eggs.
5. Take the egg out when there is not any more fluid.
6. Put one teaspoon of oil to a similar wok.
7. Cook garlic and carrots on medium warmth.
8. Mix in the eggs mixture.
9. Top with spring onion prior to serving.

1.13 Wok scrambled Egg with Prawns

Preparation time: 10 minutes
Cooking Time: 20 minutes
Serving: 4

Ingredients:
- Asian Sesame oil, two tbsp.
- Chopped garlic, two tsp.
- Green onions, three tbsp.
- Bell pepper strips, half cup
- Worcestershire sauce, two tbsp.
- Vegetable oil, two tbsp.
- Soy sauce, two tbsp.

- Salt to taste
- Bean sprouts, half cup
- Black pepper to taste
- Shrimps, two cups
- Eggs, four
- Chopped onions, two tbsp.

Instructions:
1. Warm the oil in a wok and cook the garlic and onions.
2. Add the shrimps and cook the on medium-high warmth for several seconds or until they begin to take on a changed tone.
3. Add in the bell peppers and bean sprouts cook until delicate however to some degree crispy.
4. Turn down the warmth and pour the beaten eggs and leave to set for a couple of moments.
5. At the point when the entirety of the egg has set, tip in the soy sauce and Worcestershire sauce and let it sizzle for a couple of moments.
6. Season with some salt and pepper.
7. Your dish is ready to be served.

1.14 Wok Beef and Broccoli Omelette

Preparation time: 15 minutes

Cooking Time: 30 minutes

Serving: 4

Ingredients:

- Fish sauce, two tbsp.
- Chopped garlic, two tsp.
- Green onions, three tbsp.
- Beef, one cup
- Chopped fresh dill, two tbsp.
- Vegetable oil, two tbsp.
- Soy sauce, two tbsp.
- Salt to taste
- Black pepper to taste
- Broccoli, one cup
- Eggs, twelve

Instructions:

1. Join all the fixings in little bowl.
2. Join eggs and sauces in medium bowl; beat delicately.
3. Add a large portion of the broccoli and beef combination to egg blend.
4. Warm a fourth of the vegetable oil in wok.
5. At the point when oil is simply smoking, add a fourth of the egg combination.
6. At the point when omelet is practically set, sprinkle a fourth of the leftover beef and broccoli.
7. Cook briefly, turning the omelet fifty-fifty.

8. Serve your dish with different sauces.

1.15 Wok Ham and Egg Fried Rice

Preparation time: 10 minutes
Cooking Time: 10 minutes
Serving: 4

Ingredients:
- Soy sauce, two tbsp.
- Chopped garlic, two tsp.
- Green onions, three tbsp.
- Ham slices, half cup
- Vegetable oil, two tbsp.
- Salt to taste
- Black pepper to taste
- Cooked rice, two cups
- Eggs, four

Instructions:
1. Warm a wok.
2. Add about a tablespoon of oil.
3. Add the eggs.
4. Add the diced or cut ham and mix until daintily cooked.
5. Add the ginger and garlic to the bacon.

6. Add your rice, somewhat more oil in the event that you need it and mix.
7. Add about a teaspoon of soy sauce and return the eggs to the wok.
8. Plate and serve quickly with more soy sauce.

1.16 Wok Ground Lamb and Eggs

Preparation time: 15 minutes
Cooking Time: 30 minutes
Serving: 4

Ingredients:
- Fish sauce, two tbsp.
- Chopped garlic, two tsp.
- Green onions, three tbsp.
- Ground lamb, one cup
- Chopped fresh dill, two tbsp.
- Vegetable oil, two tbsp.
- Soy sauce, two tbsp.
- Salt to taste
- Black pepper to taste
- Eggs, twelve

Instructions:
1. Join all the fixings in little bowl.

2. Join eggs and sauces in medium bowl; beat delicately.
3. Add a large portion of the lamb eat to egg blend.
4. Warm a fourth of the vegetable oil in wok.
5. At the point when oil is simply smoking, add a fourth of the egg combination.
6. At the point when omelet is practically set, sprinkle salt and pepper on top.
7. Cook briefly, turning the omelet fifty-fifty.
8. Serve your dish with different sauces.

Chapter 2: The World of Wok Lunch Recipes

This chapter contains amazing and easy to make lunch recipes using a wok. Following are some recipes below:

2.1 Wok Firecracker Chicken

Preparation time: 20 minutes

Cooking Time: 45 minutes

Serving: 4

Ingredients:

- Buffalo sauce, half cup
- Boneless chicken, two pounds
- Vinegar, one tbsp.
- Salt to taste
- Pepper to taste
- Red chili flakes, as required
- Cornstarch, half cup
- Brown sugar, half cup
- Eggs, two
- Vegetable oil, quarter cup

Instructions:
1. Preheat the wok.
2. Add nonstick spray into the wok.
3. Mix all the ingredients together.
4. Add the chicken mixture into the wok.
5. Cook properly for thirty minutes until the chicken cubes turn crispy and crunchy.
6. Dish out your chicken and serve it with any sauce you prefer.
7. Your dish is ready to be served.

2.2 Wok Chicken Chowmein

Preparation time: 25 minutes

Cooking Time: 15 minutes

Serving: 4

Ingredients:
- Chopped garlic, two tsp.
- Green onions, three tbsp.
- Bell pepper strips, half cup
- Chowmein noodles, two cups
- Chopped ginger, two tbsp.
- Vegetable oil, two tbsp.
- Soy sauce, two tbsp.
- Salt to taste
- Black pepper to taste

- Chicken cubes, two cups

Instructions:
1. Cook the chowmein noodles as per the course.
2. Channel the noodles whenever they are cooked.
3. Warm the wok over high warmth.
4. In a little bowl whisk together the wet fixings.
5. Add the oil, once hot add the garlic, chicken, and ginger.
6. Add the remainder of the vegetables and cook them until they are done.
7. Add the cooked noodles and sauce.
8. Mix to consolidate and cook until the sauce has thickened.
9. Add the chicken back to the wok.
10. Your dish is fit to be served.

2.3 Wok Cabbage Stir-Fry

Preparation time: 10 minutes
Cooking Time: 5 minutes
Serving: 4

Ingredients:
- Asian Sesame oil, two tbsp.
- Chopped garlic, two tsp.
- Cooking wine, half cup

- Soy sauce, two tbsp.
- Salt to taste
- Black pepper to taste
- Shredded cabbage, two cups

Instructions:
1. Heat a wok on medium flame.
2. Add the oil and garlic.
3. Cook the garlic, once browned add the cabbage and cooking wine into it.
4. After the cabbage is wilted and half cooked, add the soy sauce, salt, and pepper.
5. Cook for further ten minutes.
6. Your dish is ready to be served.

2.4 Wok Beef Pho

Preparation time: 25 minutes

Cooking Time: 15 minutes

Serving: 4

Ingredients:
- Soy sauce, one and a half tbsp.
- Vegetable oil, half cup
- White vinegar, a quarter cup
- Long red chili, one

- Garlic cloves, ten
- Rice noodles, one cup
- Beef, half pound
- Scallions, to serve
- Garlic cloves, four
- White peppercorns, one tsp.
- Cilantro, one cup
- Fresh ginger, one tsp.
- Fish sauce, one tbsp.
- Chicken stock, two cups

Instructions:
1. Heat a wok on medium flame.
2. Cook the beef in oil and keep aside.
3. Cook the rice noodles.
4. Combine rest of the fixings and cover it to stew for fifty minutes.
5. Presently add the soup in a bowl then add the rice noodles and beef strips.
6. Add the cilantro on top.
7. Your dish is fit to be served.

2.5 Wok Seared Salmon

Preparation time: 25 minutes

Cooking Time: 15 minutes

Serving: 4

Ingredients:
- Oyster sauce, two tbsp.
- Chopped garlic, two tsp.
- Rice wine, two tbsp.
- Mix vegetables, half cup
- Salmon, two cups
- Cajun seasoning, two tbsp.
- Vegetable oil, two tbsp.
- Soy sauce, two tbsp.
- Salt to taste
- Black pepper to taste
- Tomatoes, two cups
- Chopped onions, two tbsp.

Instructions:
1. Coat the seasoning on top of the salmon filet.
2. Heat a wok.
3. Add the oil and start cooking the salmon filet until it turns a little crispy.

4. Remove the salmon and add the onions and garlic into the wok.
5. After cooking the onions add the rest of the vegetables.
6. Add the remaining ingredients and cook for five minutes.
7. Add the salmon filet into the mixture.
8. Cook for five minutes.
9. Your dish is ready to be served.

2.6 Wok Fried Shrimp with Garlic

Preparation time: 25 minutes

Cooking Time: 15 minutes

Serving: 4

Ingredients:
- Asian Sesame oil, two tbsp.
- Chopped garlic, two tsp.
- Shrimps, two pounds
- Salt to taste
- Black pepper to taste

Instructions:
1. Heat a large wok.
2. Add the vegetable oil and heat it over high for a few minutes.
3. Add in the garlic and let it brown.

4. Add in the shrimps and cook it for two minutes.
5. Season generously with kosher salt and pepper.
6. Cook for five more minutes.
7. Your dish is ready to be served.

2.7 Wok Fried Malaysian Noodles

Preparation time: 15 minutes
Cooking Time: 15 minutes
Serving: 4

Ingredients:
- Asian Sesame oil, two tbsp.
- Chopped garlic, two tsp.
- Maggi seasoning, three tbsp.
- Scallions, half cup
- Rice noodles, two cups
- Shrimps, one pound
- Vegetable oil, two tbsp.
- Soy sauce, two tbsp.
- Salt to taste
- Black pepper to taste
- Bean sprouts, two cups
- Eggs, two
- Sausages, one cup

Instructions:

1. Cook the rice noodles according to the package instructions.
2. Warm a wok over high warmth for a couple of moments.
3. Coat wok with vegetable oil.
4. Add shrimp and garlic.
5. Cook the sausage until it starts to brown.
6. Add eggs into the wok.
7. Mix everything together, add noodles, and delicately blend.
8. Add Maggi Seasoning and rest of the ingredients.
9. Cook for five minutes.
10. Your dish is ready to be served.

2.8 Wok Fried Macaroni

Preparation time: 25 minutes

Cooking Time: 15 minutes

Serving: 4

Ingredients:

- Asian Sesame oil, two tbsp.
- Chopped garlic, two tsp.
- Maggi seasoning, three tbsp.
- Scallions, half cup

- Macaroni, two cups
- Shrimps, one pound
- Vegetable oil, two tbsp.
- Soy sauce, two tbsp.
- Salt to taste
- Black pepper to taste
- Bean sprouts, two cups
- Sausages, one cup

Instructions:

1. Cook the macaroni according to the package instructions.
2. Warm a wok over high warmth for a couple of moments.
3. Coat wok with vegetable oil.
4. Add shrimp and garlic.
5. Cook the sausage until it starts to brown.
6. Mix everything, add macaroni, and delicately blend.
7. Add Maggi Seasoning and rest of the ingredients.
8. Cook for five minutes.
9. Your dish is ready to be served.

2.9 Wok Peanuts and Chicken

Preparation time: 10 minutes
Cooking Time: 5 minutes
Serving: 4

Ingredients:
- Soy sauce, two tbsp.
- Peanuts, two cups
- Chicken, two pounds
- Vegetable oil, two tbsp.
- Cornstarch, two tbsp.
- Sesame oil, two tbsp.
- Sugar, one tsp.
- Oyster sauce, two tbsp.
- Pepper to taste
- Salt, as required
- Chinese cooking wine, two tsp.

Instructions:
1. Add the oil in a wok.
2. Add in the chicken and cook it properly.
3. Remove the chicken from the wok.
4. Next add the peanuts and cook it.
5. Add the chicken and rest of the ingredients.

6. In the end add the cornstarch and when the dish thickens switch off the heat.
7. Your dish is ready to be served.

2.10 Wok Smoked Salmon

Preparation time: 25 minutes
Cooking Time: 15 minutes
Serving: 4

Ingredients:
- Asian Sesame oil, two tbsp.
- Chopped garlic, two tsp.
- Salmon filet, two pounds
- Chopped fresh dill, two tbsp.
- Vegetable oil, two tbsp.
- Soy sauce, two tbsp.
- Salt to taste
- Black pepper to taste
- Oyster sauce, two tbsp.
- Aluminum foil, as required

Instructions:
1. Mix all the ingredients together.
2. Spread it all over the salmon filet.
3. Let the mixture soak up in the salmon filet.

4. Cover the filet in the aluminum foil.
5. Line a wok with coal at the bottom.
6. Place it inside a wok and cover it.
7. Let the salmon cook for fifteen minutes.
8. Your dish is ready to be served.

2.11 Wok Broccoli with Oyster Sauce

Preparation time: 10 minutes

Cooking Time: 5 minutes

Serving: 4

Ingredients:
- Asian Sesame oil, two tbsp.
- Chopped garlic, two tsp.
- Cooking wine, half cup
- Soy sauce, two tbsp.
- Oyster sauce, two tbsp.
- Salt to taste
- Black pepper to taste
- Broccoli, two cups

Instructions:
1. Heat a wok on medium flame.
2. Add oil and garlic.

3. Cook the garlic, once browned, add the broccoli and cooking wine into it.
4. After the broccoli is wilted and half cooked, add the soy sauce, oyster sauce, salt, and pepper.
5. Cook for further ten minutes.
6. Your dish is ready to be served.

2.12 Wok Mongolian Chicken

Preparation time: 20 minutes

Cooking Time: 45 minutes

Serving: 4

Ingredients:
- Boneless chicken, two pounds
- Vinegar, one tbsp.
- Salt to taste
- Pepper to taste
- Green onions, half cup
- Cornstarch, half cup
- Brown sugar, half cup
- Eggs, two
- Soy sauce, half cup
- Vegetable oil, quarter cup

Instructions:

1. Preheat the wok.
2. Add nonstick spray into the wok.
3. Mix all the ingredients together.
4. Add the chicken mixture into the wok.
5. Cook properly for thirty minutes until the chicken cubes turn crispy and crunchy.
6. Dish out your chicken and serve it with any sauce you prefer.
7. Your dish is ready to be served.

2.13 Wok Almond Vegetable Stir Fry

Preparation time: 10 minutes

Cooking Time: 5 minutes

Serving: 4

Ingredients:
- Soy sauce, two tbsp.
- Almonds, one cup
- Mix vegetables, two cups
- Vegetable oil, two tbsp.
- Cornstarch, two tbsp.
- Sesame oil, two tbsp.
- Sugar, one tsp.
- Oyster sauce, two tbsp.
- Pepper to taste
- Salt, as required

- Chinese cooking wine, two tsp.

Instructions:
1. Add the oil in a wok.
2. Add in the almonds and cook it properly.
3. Remove the almonds from the wok.
4. Next add the mixed vegetables and cook it.
5. Add the rest of the ingredients.
6. In the end add the cornstarch and when the dish thickens switch off the heat.
7. Your dish is ready to be served.

2.14 Wok Sweet and Sour Beef

Preparation time: 10 minutes

Cooking Time: 10 minutes

Serving: 4

Ingredients:
- Asian Sesame oil, two tbsp.
- Chopped garlic, two tsp.
- Green onions, three tbsp.
- Broccoli, half cup
- Beef cubes, two cups
- Chopped shallots, two tbsp.
- Vegetable oil, two tbsp.
- Soy sauce, two tbsp.

- Salt to taste
- Black pepper to taste
- Stir-fry sweet and sour sauce, two cups
- Chopped onions, two tbsp.

Instructions:

1. In a wok, add oil and heat it.
2. Add in the beef cubes and let it cook for five minutes.
3. Remove the cubes of beef once they are cooked.
4. Add the chopped onions in the wok.
5. Add in the vegetables and let them cook.
6. Once cooked, add in the rest of the ingredients.
7. Add the beef cubes.
8. Bring to boil and then turn off the flame.
9. Your dish is ready to be served.

2.15 Wok Turkey Asparagus Stir-Fry

Preparation time: 10 minutes

Cooking Time: 5 minutes

Serving: 4

Ingredients:

- Soy sauce, two tbsp.
- Asparagus, two cups
- Turkey strips, two pounds
- Vegetable oil, two tbsp.
- Cornstarch, two tbsp.
- Sesame oil, two tbsp.
- Sugar, one tsp.
- Oyster sauce, two tbsp.
- Pepper to taste
- Salt, as required
- Chinese cooking wine, two tsp.

Instructions:
1. Add the oil in a wok.
2. Add in the turkey strips and cook it properly.
3. Remove the turkey strips from the wok.
4. Next add the asparagus and cook it.
5. Add the turkey and rest of the ingredients.
6. In the end add the cornstarch and when the dish thickens switch off the heat.
7. Your dish is ready to be served.

2.16 Wok Snappy Chicken Stir -Fry

Preparation time: 10 minutes

Cooking Time: 5 minutes

Serving: 4

> **Ingredients:**
> - Asian Sesame oil, two tbsp.
> - Chopped garlic, two tsp.
> - Cooking wine, half cup
> - Soy sauce, two tbsp.
> - Salt to taste
> - Black pepper to taste
> - Chicken cubes, two cups

Instructions:
1. Heat a wok on medium flame.
2. Add the oil and garlic.
3. Cook the garlic, once browned add the chicken and add wine into it.
4. After the chicken is half cooked, add the soy sauce, salt, and pepper.
5. Cook for further ten minutes.
6. Your dish is ready to be served.

Chapter 3: The World of Wok Dinner Recipes

This chapter contains amazing and easy to make dinner recipes using a wok. Following are some recipes below:

3.1 Wok Coconut Shrimp Curry

Preparation time: 25 minutes

Cooking Time: 25 minutes

Serving: 4

Ingredients:
- Asian Sesame oil, two tbsp.
- Chopped garlic, two tsp.
- Green onions, three tbsp.
- Bell pepper strips, half cup
- Coconut milk, two cups
- Chopped fresh dill, two tbsp.
- Vegetable oil, two tbsp.
- Soy sauce, two tbsp.
- Salt to taste
- Shrimps, two pounds
- Black pepper to taste
- Carrots, two cups
- Bean sprouts, one cup

- Peas, one cup
- Shredded coconut, as required
- Chopped onions, two tbsp.

Instructions:
1. In a large wok, add the oil and heat it.
2. Add garlic and shrimps into the oil.
3. Let it cook and then remove it from the wok.
4. Add in the onions and fry it.
5. Add the vegetables and cook for a few minutes.
6. Add the sauces and coconut milk into the wok and bring to boil.
7. Add in the shrimps.
8. Cook for ten minutes.
9. Garnish with shredded coconut and shallots.
10. Your dish is ready to be served.

3.2 Wok Mandarin Pork Stir-Fry

Preparation time: 25 minutes

Cooking Time: 15 minutes

Serving: 4

Ingredients:
- Asian Sesame oil, two tbsp.

- Chopped garlic, two tsp.
- Orange juice, three tbsp.
- Cornstarch, half cup
- Pork, two cups
- Water, two tbsp.
- Vegetable oil, two tbsp.
- Soy sauce, two tbsp.
- Salt to taste
- Black pepper to taste
- Rice, two cups
- Peas, one cup
- Ginger powder, two tbsp.

Instructions:
1. Cook rice as indicated by bundle.
2. Then, in a little bowl, join the cornstarch, garlic powder and ginger.
3. Mix in squeezed orange until smooth.
4. Mix in water and soy sauce; put in a safe spot.
5. In an enormous wok, pan sear pork in oil until juices run clear.
6. In a similar wok, cook peas until delicate.
7. Return pork to wok.
8. Mix squeezed orange blend; add to wok.
9. Cook and mix for a few minutes or until thickened.
10. Tenderly mix in oranges.

11. Present with rice.
12. Your dish is ready to be served.

3.3 Wok Asparagus Tofu Stir-Fry

Preparation time: 10 minutes
Cooking Time: 5 minutes
Serving: 4

Ingredients:
- Soy sauce, two tbsp.
- Asparagus, two cups
- Tofu cubes, two pounds
- Vegetable oil, two tbsp.
- Cornstarch, two tbsp.
- Sesame oil, two tbsp.
- Sugar, one tsp.
- Oyster sauce, two tbsp.
- Pepper to taste
- Salt, as required
- Chinese cooking wine, two tsp.

Instructions:
1. Add the oil in a wok.

2. Add in the tofu cubes and cook it properly.
3. Remove the tofu cubes from the wok.
4. Next add the asparagus and cook it.
5. Add the tofu cubes and rest of the ingredients.
6. In the end, add the cornstarch and when the dish thickens switch off the heat.
7. Your dish is ready to be served.

3.4 Wok Balsamic Pork Stir-Fry

Preparation time: 25 minutes

Cooking Time: 15 minutes

Serving: 4

Ingredients:
- Asian Sesame oil, two tbsp.
- Chopped garlic, two tsp.
- Balsamic vinegar, three tbsp.
- Cornstarch, half cup
- Pork, two cups
- Water, two tbsp.
- Vegetable oil, two tbsp.
- Soy sauce, two tbsp.
- Salt to taste
- Black pepper to taste
- Rice, two cups

- Peas, one cup
- Ginger powder, two tbsp.

Instructions:
1. Cook rice as indicated by bundle.
2. Then, in a little bowl, join the cornstarch, garlic powder and ginger.
3. Mix in the balsamic vinegar until smooth.
4. Mix in water and soy sauce; put in a safe spot.
5. In an enormous wok, pan sear pork in oil until juices run clear.
6. In a similar wok, cook peas until delicate.
7. Return pork to wok.
8. Mix in the above formed blend.
9. Cook and mix for a few minutes or until thickened.
10. Tenderly mix in oranges.
11. Present with rice.
12. Your dish is ready to be served.

3.5 Wok Beef Orange Stir-Fry

Preparation time: 30 minutes

Cooking Time: 10 minutes

Serving: 4

Ingredients:
- Sesame oil, one tsp.

- Cornstarch, a quarter cup
- Beef cubes, one pound
- Dried orange peel, one tsp.
- Orange juice, a quarter cup
- Soy sauce, one tbsp.
- Garlic powder, half tsp.
- White pepper, a quarter tsp.
- Shaoxing wine, two tbsp.
- Dried chili pepper, six
- Beef stock, a quarter cup
- Sugar, two tbsp.
- Star anise, two
- Tangerine peel, two

Instructions:
1. Mix the beef in the sesame oil, white pepper, garlic powder, salt, and Shaoxing wine in a wok.
2. Dredge the beef pieces in cornstarch and fry until golden.
3. Heat a wok over medium heat and add a tablespoon of oil.
4. Add the dried chili peppers, tangerine peel, and star anise, and toast for about twenty seconds, being careful not to burn the aromatics.
5. Add the orange juice, beef stock, vinegar, sugar, and soy sauce.

6. Bring the sauce to a simmer and gradually add the cornstarch slurry, stirring constantly.
7. Mix all the things.
8. Your dish is ready to be served.

3.6 Wok Sizzling Chicken Lo Mein

Preparation time: 25 minutes
Cooking Time: 15 minutes
Serving: 4

Ingredients:
- Asian Sesame oil, two tbsp.
- Chopped garlic, two tsp.
- Green onions, three tbsp.
- Linguine noodles, two cup
- Chicken cubes, two cups
- Chopped fresh dill, two tbsp.
- Teriyaki sauce, two tbsp.
- Soy sauce, two tbsp.
- Salt to taste
- Black pepper to taste
- Mix vegetables, two cups
- Chopped onions, two tbsp.

Instructions:

1. Cook the noodles according to package directions.
2. Meanwhile, in a large wok, stir-fry chicken in oil until no longer pink.
3. Add stir fry sauce and teriyaki sauce.
4. Remove chicken from the wok.
5. Stir-fry the vegetables until they are crisp-tender.
6. Drain the noodles.
7. Add the noodles, chicken and remaining sauces to the wok.
8. Your dish is ready to be served.

3.7 Wok Chicken Soba Noodle Toss

Preparation time: 25 minutes

Cooking Time: 15 minutes

Serving: 4

Ingredients:
- Hoisin sauce, two tbsp.
- Chopped garlic, two tsp.
- Corn starch, three tbsp.
- Chicken broth, half cup
- Mix vegetables, two cups
- Brown sugar, two tbsp.
- Vegetable oil, two tbsp.
- Soy sauce, two tbsp.
- Salt to taste

- Black pepper to taste
- Noodles two cups
- Chicken cubes, one pound
- Chopped onions, two tbsp.

Instructions:
1. In a small bowl, combine the cloves, brown sugar, corn starch, soy sauce, hoisin sauce, ginger, and chicken broth until blended.
2. Cook the noodles according to package directions.
3. In a large wok, stir-fry chicken in the oil until they turn white.
4. Stir-fry the vegetables in remaining oil until they are crisp-tender.
5. Stir cornstarch mixture.
6. Bring to a boil; cook until thickened.
7. Add all the ingredients into the wok.
8. Your dish is ready to be served.

3.8 Wok Peking Shrimp

Preparation time: 25 minutes

Cooking Time: 15 minutes

Serving: 4

Ingredients:
- Asian Sesame oil, two tbsp.

- Chopped garlic, two tsp.
- Chopped ginger, three tbsp.
- Chicken stock, half cup
- Rice, two cups
- Corn syrup, two tbsp.
- Vegetable oil, two tbsp.
- Soy sauce, two tbsp.
- Salt to taste
- Black pepper to taste
- Shrimps, two cups
- Cornstarch, two tbsp.

Instructions:
1. In a little bowl, join cornstarch and water until smooth.
2. Mix in the corn syrup, soy sauce, sherry or stock, garlic, and ginger and put in a safe spot.
3. In a nonstick wok, add green pepper in hot oil.
4. Add the shrimps and cook until shrimps turn pink.
5. Mix in the cornstarch combination and add to the dish.
6. Heat to the point of boiling and cook until sauce is thickened.
7. Add the tomato.
8. Present with rice if wanted.

9. Your dish is ready to be served.

3.9 Wok Curried Fried Rice with Pineapple

Preparation time: 10 minutes
Cooking Time: 10 minutes
Serving: 4

Ingredients:
- Soy sauce, two tbsp.
- Chopped garlic, two tsp.
- Green onions, three tbsp.
- Bacon strips, half cup
- Vegetable oil, two tbsp.
- Salt to taste
- Black pepper to taste
- Cooked rice, two cups
- Eggs, four
- Pineapple chunks, one cup

Instructions:
1. Warm a wok.
2. Add about a tablespoon of oil.
3. Add the eggs.
4. Add the diced or cut bacon and mix ntil daintily cooked.

5. Add the ginger and garlic to the bacon.
6. Add your rice, somewhat more oil in the event that you need it and mix.
7. Add about a teaspoon of soy sauce and return the eggs to the wok.
8. Add the pineapple chunks.
9. Plate and serve quickly with more soy sauce.

3.10 Wok Ginger Peach Pork

Preparation time: 25 minutes

Cooking Time: 15 minutes

Serving: 4

Ingredients:
- Asian Sesame oil, two tbsp.
- Chopped garlic, two tsp.
- Ginger, three tbsp.
- Cornstarch, half cup
- Pork, two cups
- Water, two tbsp.
- Vegetable oil, two tbsp.
- Soy sauce, two tbsp.
- Salt to taste
- Black pepper to taste
- Rice, two cups
- Peach cubes, one cup

Instructions:

1. Cook rice as indicated by the bundle.
2. Then, in a little bowl, join the cornstarch, garlic powder and ginger.
3. Mix in peach cubes until smooth.
4. Mix in water and soy sauce; put in a safe spot.
5. In an enormous wok, cook pork in oil until juices run clear.
6. Return pork to wok.
7. Mix the above formed blend and add it to the wok.
8. Cook and mix for a few minutes or until thickened.
9. Tenderly mix in everything.
10. Present with rice.
11. Your dish is ready to be served.

3.11 Wok Nutty Chicken Fried Rice

Preparation time: 10 minutes

Cooking Time: 10 minutes

Serving: 4

Ingredients:

- Soy sauce, two tbsp.
- Chopped garlic, two tsp.

- Green onions, three tbsp.
- Chicken strips, half cup
- Vegetable oil, two tbsp.
- Salt to taste
- Black pepper to taste
- Cooked rice, two cups
- Eggs, four
- Mixed nuts, one cup

Instructions:
1. Warm a wok.
2. Add about a tablespoon of oil.
3. Add the eggs.
4. Add the diced or cut chicken and mix until daintily cooked.
5. Add the ginger and garlic to the chicken.
6. Add your rice, somewhat more oil in the event that you need it and mix.
7. Add about a teaspoon of soy sauce and return the eggs to the wok.
8. Add the mixed nuts.
9. Your dish is ready to be served.

3.12 Wok Honey Garlic Chicken Stir-Fry

Preparation time: 25 minutes

Cooking Time: 15 minutes

Serving: 4

Ingredients:

- Asian Sesame oil, two tbsp.
- Chopped garlic, two tsp.
- Chicken, two pounds
- Salt to taste
- Black pepper to taste
- Honey, two tbsp.

Instructions:

1. Heat a large wok.
2. Add the vegetable oil and heat it over high for a few minutes.
3. Add in the garlic and let it brown.
4. Add in the chicken and cook it for two minutes.
5. Season generously with kosher salt and pepper.
6. Add in the honey and mix well.
7. Cook for five more minutes.
8. Your dish is ready to be served.

3.13 Wok Chicken Teriyaki

Preparation time: 30 minutes
Cooking Time: 10 minutes
Serving: 4

Ingredients:
- Sesame oil, one tsp.
- Cornstarch, a quarter cup
- Chicken cubes, one pound
- Teriyaki sauce, a quarter cup
- Soy sauce, one tbsp.
- Garlic powder, half tsp.
- White pepper, a quarter tsp.
- Shaoxing wine, two tbsp.
- Dried chili pepper, six
- Chicken stock, a quarter cup
- Sugar, two tbsp.
- Star anise, two
- Tangerine peel, two

Instructions:
1. Mix the chicken in the sesame oil, white pepper, garlic powder, salt, and Shaoxing wine in a wok.

2. Dredge the chicken pieces in cornstarch and fry until golden.
3. Heat a wok over medium heat and add a tablespoon of oil.
4. Add the dried chili peppers, tangerine peel, and star anise, and toast for about twenty seconds, being careful not to burn the aromatics.
5. Add the teriyaki sauce, chicken stock, vinegar, sugar, and soy sauce.
6. Bring the sauce to a simmer and gradually add the cornstarch slurry, stirring constantly.
7. Mix all the things.
8. Your dish is ready to be served.

3.14 Wok Honey Soy Wings

Preparation time: 25 minutes

Cooking Time: 15 minutes

Serving: 4

Ingredients:
- Asian Sesame oil, two tbsp.
- Chopped garlic, two tsp.
- Chicken wings, two pounds
- Salt to taste
- Black pepper to taste
- Honey, two tbsp.

Instructions:

1. Heat a large wok.
2. Add the vegetable oil and heat it over high for a few minutes.
3. Add in the garlic and let it brown.
4. Add in the chicken wings and cook it for two minutes.
5. Season generously with kosher salt and pepper.
6. Add in the honey and mix well.
7. Cook for five more minutes.
8. Your dish is ready to be served.

3.15 Wok Lime and Chili Chicken

Preparation time: 30 minutes

Cooking Time: 10 minutes

Serving: 4

Ingredients:

- Sesame oil, one tsp.
- Cornstarch, a quarter cup
- Chicken cubes, one pound
- Soy sauce, one tbsp.
- Garlic powder, half tsp.

- White pepper, a quarter tsp.
- Lime juice, two tbsp.
- Dried chili pepper, six
- Chicken stock, a quarter cup
- Sugar, two tbsp.
- Star anise, two
- Tangerine peel, two

Instructions:
1. Mix the chicken in the sesame oil, white pepper, garlic powder, salt, and lime juice in a wok.
2. Dredge the chicken pieces in cornstarch and fry until golden.
3. Heat a wok over medium heat and add a tablespoon of oil.
4. Add the dried chili peppers, tangerine peel, and star anise, and toast for about twenty seconds, being careful not to burn the aromatics.
5. Add the chicken stock, vinegar, sugar, and soy sauce.
6. Bring the sauce to a simmer and gradually add the cornstarch slurry, stirring constantly.
7. Mix all the things together.
8. Your dish is ready to be served.

3.16 Wok Potato and Chicken Stir-Fry

Preparation time: 10 minutes
Cooking Time: 5 minutes
Serving: 4

Ingredients:
- Soy sauce, two tbsp.
- Potatoes, two cups
- Chicken, two pounds
- Vegetable oil, two tbsp.
- Cornstarch, two tbsp.
- Sesame oil, two tbsp.
- Sugar, one tsp.
- Oyster sauce, two tbsp.
- Pepper to taste
- Salt, as required
- Chinese cooking wine, two tsp.

Instructions:
1. Add the oil in a wok.
2. Add in the chicken and cook it properly.
3. Remove the chicken from the wok.
4. Next, add the potatoes and cook it.
5. Add the chicken and rest of the ingredients.

6. In the end, add the cornstarch and once the dish thickens, switch off the heat.
7. Your dish is ready to be served.

Chapter 4: The World of Wok Snack Recipes

This chapter contains amazing and easy to make snack recipes using a wok. Following are some recipes:

4.1 Wok Fried Prawn Crackers

Preparation time: 25 minutes

Cooking Time: 15 minutes

Serving: 4

Ingredients:
- Asian Sesame oil, two tbsp.
- Chopped garlic, two tsp.
- Green onions, three tbsp.
- Vegetable oil, half cup
- Prawns, two cups
- Chopped fresh dill, two tbsp.
- Soy sauce, two tbsp.
- Salt to taste
- Black pepper to taste
- Flour, one cup
- Egg, one
- Chopped onions, two tbsp.

Instructions:

1. Mix the chopped garlic, prawns, sesame oil, soy sauce, salt, and pepper together in a bowl.
2. Beat the egg in a separate bowl.
3. Dip the prawns in the egg and then cover with flour.
4. Fry these prawns in a large wok with added oil.
5. Once fried, remove from the wok.
6. Add fresh onion, and dill on top.
7. Your dish is ready to be served.

4.2 Wok Popcorn

Preparation time: 25 minutes

Cooking Time: 10 minutes

Serving: 4

Ingredients:

- Butter, one tbsp.
- Vegetable oil, two tbsp.
- Corn kernels, two tbsp.
- Salt, as preferred

Instructions:
1. Heat a large wok until it starts smoking.
2. Add in the oil and corn kernels.
3. Add salt as preferred.
4. After a few minutes, add in the butter.
5. Cover the wok for a few minutes.
6. You will hear popping sounds.
7. When the sound stops, it's time to switch off the stove.
8. Your dish is ready to be served.

4.3 Wok Egg Rolls

Preparation time: 25 minutes
Cooking Time: 15 minutes
Serving: 4

Ingredients:
- Asian Sesame oil, two tbsp.
- Chopped garlic, two tsp.
- Green onions, three tbsp.
- Mix vegetables, half cup
- Chopped fresh dill, two tbsp.
- Vegetable oil, as required
- Soy sauce, to serve
- Salt to taste
- Black pepper to taste

- Eggs, six
- Wonton wraps, as required
- Water, as required

Instructions:
1. In a wok, add one tablespoon of oil.
2. Let it heat up and then add eggs into it.
3. Scramble the eggs.
4. Add salt and pepper.
5. Add in the mixed vegetables and cook for two minutes.
6. When cooked, add the egg mixture into a bowl.
7. Add the prepared mixture into the wonton wrappers and fold them into a roll.
8. Fry the rolls in a small amount of oil in the wok.
9. Serve your egg rolls with soy sauce or any other sauce that you may prefer.

4.4 Wok Chili Bamboo Shoots

Preparation time: 25 minutes
Cooking Time: 15 minutes

Serving: 4

Ingredients:
- Asian Sesame oil, two tbsp.
- Chopped garlic, two tsp.
- Bamboo shoots, two cups
- White pepper, two tbsp.
- Vegetable oil, two tbsp.
- Chili oil, two tbsp.
- Salt to taste
- Black pepper to taste

Instructions:
1. Cut the bamboo shoots into a small thin thread-like structures.
2. Wash the bamboo shoots properly.
3. Dry your bamboo shoots with the help of a towel.
4. Once dried, transfer them into a bowl.
5. Mix in the rest of the ingredients.
6. You can store your bamboo shoots as well for a couple of days.
7. Your dish is ready to be served.

4.5 Wok Scallion Pancakes

Preparation time: 25 minutes
Cooking Time: 15 minutes

Serving: 4

Ingredients

- Chopped garlic, two tsp.
- Green onions, three tbsp.
- Chopped fresh scallions, half cup
- Butter, two tbsp.
- Salt to taste
- Baking soda, one tsp.
- Black pepper to taste
- Flour, two cups
- Eggs, two
- Chopped onions, two tbsp.
- Milk, one cup

Instructions:

1. In a large bowl sift the flour well.
2. Add in the fresh scallions, green onions, chopped garlic, baking soda, chopped onions, salt, and pepper.
3. In a separate bowl, mix in the milk and eggs together.
4. Add the milk and egg mixture into the dried mixture.
5. Mix delicately until a smooth texture is formed.
6. In a wok, add the butter and scoop in some amount of the pancake batter.

7. Cook the batter and flip it making sure both the sides are cooked properly.
8. Your dish is ready to be served.

4.6 Wok Stuffed Mushrooms

Preparation time: 25 minutes
Cooking Time: 15 minutes
Serving: 4

Ingredients:
- Asian Sesame oil, two tbsp.
- Chopped garlic, two tsp.
- Green onions, three tbsp.
- Mozzarella cheese, half cup
- Mixed vegetables, two cups
- Chopped fresh dill, two tbsp.
- Vegetable oil, two tbsp.
- Soy sauce, two tbsp.
- Salt to taste
- Black pepper to taste
- Mushrooms, two cups
- Chopped onions, two tbsp.

Instructions:

1. In a bowl mix the mozzarella cheese, mixed vegetables, chopped garlic, green onions, salt, pepper, chopped onions, soy sauce, fresh dill, and sesame oil together.
2. Remove the inner sides of the mushroom.
3. Add the above-formed mixture into the mushrooms filling it completely.
4. In a large wok, place these filled mushrooms.
5. Spray non-stick cooking spray.
6. Cover the wok and let it cook for ten minutes.
7. Your dish is ready to be served.

4.7 Wok Zucchini Pancakes

Preparation time: 25 minutes

Cooking Time: 15 minutes

Serving: 4

Ingredients

- Chopped garlic, two tsp.
- Green onions, three tbsp.
- Chopped fresh zucchini, half cup
- Butter, two tbsp.
- Salt to taste
- Baking soda, one tsp.
- Black pepper to taste
- Flour, two cups
- Eggs, two

- Chopped onions, two tbsp.
- Milk, one cup

Instructions:

1. In a large bowl sift the flour well.
2. Add in the fresh zucchini, green onions, chopped garlic, baking soda, chopped onions, salt and pepper.
3. In a separate bowl mix in the milk, and eggs together.
4. Add the milk and egg mixture into the dried mixture.
5. Mix delicately until smooth texture is formed.
6. In a wok, add the butter and scoop in some amount of the pancake batter.
7. Cook the batter and flip it making sure both the sides are cooked properly.
8. Your dish is ready to be served.

4.8 Wok Avocado Egg Rolls

Preparation time: 25 minutes

Cooking Time: 15 minutes

Serving: 4

Ingredients:

- Asian Sesame oil, two tbsp.

- Chopped garlic, two tsp.
- Green onions, three tbsp.
- Mix vegetables, half cup
- Chopped fresh dill, two tbsp.
- Vegetable oil, as required
- Soy sauce, to serve
- Salt to taste
- Black pepper to taste
- Eggs, six
- Avocado cubes, one cup
- Wonton wraps, as required
- Water, as required

Instructions:
1. In a wok, add one tablespoon of oil.
2. Let it heat up and then add eggs into it.
3. Scramble the eggs.
4. Add salt and pepper.
5. Add in the mixed vegetables and cook for two minutes.
6. When cooked add the egg mixture into a bowl.
7. Mix in the avocado cubes with the egg mixture.
8. Add the prepared mixture into the wonton wrappers and fold them into a roll.
9. Fry the rolls in a small amount of oil in the wok.

10. Serve your avocado egg rolls with soy sauce or any other sauce that you may prefer.

4.9 Wok Sticky Rice Dumplings

Preparation time: 25 minutes

Cooking Time: 15 minutes

Serving: 4

Ingredients:
- Asian Sesame oil, two tbsp.
- Chopped garlic, two tsp.
- Green onions, three tbsp.
- Brown sugar, half cup
- Glutinous rice, two cups
- Chopped fresh dill, two tbsp.
- Vegetable oil, two tbsp.
- Soy sauce, two tbsp.
- Salt to taste
- Black pepper to taste
- Bamboo leaves, as required

Instructions:
1. In a wok, add the sesame oil.
2. Heat the oil and add in the chopped garlic.
3. Add the glutinous rice and then add the vegetable oil.
4. Add in the brown sugar and green onions.
5. Add in the soy sauce and chopped fresh dill.

6. Cook the mixture for five minutes.
7. Season with salt and pepper.
8. When cooked remove from the heat.
9. Make the dumplings by filling a small amount of mixture in the bamboo leaves.
10. Your dish is ready to be served.

4.10 Wok Pork and Fish Dumplings

Preparation time: 25 minutes

Cooking Time: 15 minutes

Serving: 4

Ingredients:
- Asian Sesame oil, two tbsp.
- Chopped garlic, two tsp.
- Green onions, three tbsp.
- Fish mince, two cups
- Pork mince, two cups
- Chopped fresh dill, two tbsp.
- Vegetable oil, two tbsp.
- Soy sauce, two tbsp.
- Salt to taste
- Black pepper to taste
- Bamboo leaves, as required

Instructions:
1. In a wok, add the sesame oil.
2. Heat the oil and add in the chopped garlic.
3. Add the pork and fish meat, and then add the vegetable oil.
4. Add in the green onions.
5. Add in the soy sauce and chopped fresh dill.
6. Cook the mixture for five minutes.
7. Season with salt and pepper.
8. When cooked remove from the heat.
9. Make the dumplings by filling a small amount of mixture in the bamboo leaves.
10. Your dish is ready to be served.

4.11 Wok Cream Cheese Wontons

Preparation time: 25 minutes

Cooking Time: 15 minutes

Serving: 4

Ingredients:
- Wonton wraps, as required
- Oil, for frying
- Caster sugar, one cup
- Mixed nuts, two tbsp.
- Cream cheese, two cups

- Eggs, one

Instructions:

1. Mix all the ingredients together in a bowl.
2. Add the mixed nuts.
3. Add a tablespoon of the mixture in a wonton wrap and cover it with egg wash so that it forms a ball structure.
4. Fry these balls until golden brown.
5. Your dish is ready to be served.

4.12 Wok Sesame Pancakes

Preparation time: 25 minutes

Cooking Time: 15 minutes

Serving: 4

Ingredients

- Chopped garlic, two tsp.
- Green onions, three tbsp.
- Sesame seeds, half cup
- Butter, two tbsp.
- Salt to taste
- Baking soda, one tsp.
- Black pepper to taste
- Flour, two cups

- Eggs, two
- Chopped onions, two tbsp.
- Milk, one cup

Instructions:
1. In a large bowl, sift the flour well.
2. Add in the sesame seeds, green onions, chopped garlic, baking soda, chopped onions, salt and pepper.
3. In a separate bowl mix in the milk and eggs together.
4. Add the milk and egg mixture into the dried mixture.
5. Mix delicately until smooth texture is formed.
6. In a wok, add the butter and scoop in some amount of the pancake batter.
7. Cook the batter and flip it making sure both the sides are cooked properly.
8. Your dish is ready to be served.

4.13 Wok Kimchi Pancakes

Preparation time: 25 minutes

Cooking Time: 15 minutes

Serving: 4

Ingredients
- Chopped garlic, two tsp.
- Green onions, three tbsp.
- Kimchi, half cup
- Butter, two tbsp.
- Salt to taste
- Baking soda, one tsp.
- Black pepper to taste
- Flour, two cups
- Eggs, two
- Chopped onions, two tbsp.
- Milk, one cup

Instructions:
1. In a large bowl, sift the flour well.
2. Add in the kimchi, green onions, chopped garlic, baking soda, chopped onions, salt and pepper.
3. In a separate bowl mix in the milk and eggs together.
4. Add the milk and egg mixture into the dried mixture.
5. Mix delicately until smooth texture is formed.
6. In a wok, add the butter and scoop in some amount of the pancake batter.

7. Cook the batter and flip it making sure both the sides are cooked properly.
8. Your dish is ready to be served.

4.14 Wok Carrot Pancakes

Preparation time: 25 minutes
Cooking Time: 15 minutes
Serving: 4

Ingredients

- Chopped garlic, two tsp.
- Green onions, three tbsp.
- Carrots, half cup
- Butter, two tbsp.
- Salt to taste
- Baking soda, one tsp.
- Black pepper to taste
- Flour, two cups
- Eggs, two
- Chopped onions, two tbsp.
- Milk, one cup

Instructions:

1. In a large bowl, sift the flour well.

2. Add in the carrots, green onions, chopped garlic, baking soda, chopped onions, salt and pepper.
3. In a separate bowl mix in the milk, and eggs together.
4. Add the milk and egg mixture into the dried mixture.
5. Mix delicately until smooth texture is formed.
6. In a wok, add the butter and scoop in some amount of the pancake batter.
7. Cook the batter and flip it making sure both the sides are cooked properly.
8. Your dish is ready to be served.

Chapter 5: The world of wok Vegetarian recipes

This chapter contains amazing and easy to make vegetarian recipes using a wok. Following are some recipes below:

5.1 Wok Seared Tofu

Preparation time: 25 minutes

Cooking Time: 15 minutes

Serving: 4

Ingredients:
- Oyster sauce, two tbsp.
- Chopped garlic, two tsp.
- Rice wine, two tbsp.
- Mix vegetables, half cup
- Tofu cubes, two cups
- Cajun seasoning, two tbsp.
- Vegetable oil, two tbsp.
- Soy sauce, two tbsp.
- Salt to taste
- Black pepper to taste
- Tomatoes, two cups
- Chopped onions, two tbsp.

Instructions:
1. Coat the seasoning on top of the tofu cubes.
2. Heat a wok.
3. Add the oil and start cooking the tofu cubes until it turns a little crispy.
4. Remove the tofu and add the onions and garlic into the wok.
5. After cooking the onions add the rest of the vegetables.
6. Add the remaining ingredients and cook for five minutes.
7. Add the tofu blocks into the mixture.
8. Cook for five minutes.
9. Your dish is ready to be served.

5.2 Wok Vegan Yaki Udon

Preparation time: 25 minutes

Cooking Time: 15 minutes

Serving: 4

Ingredients:
- Asian Sesame oil, two tbsp.
- Chopped garlic, two tsp.
- Green onions, three tbsp.
- Udon noodles, two cup
- Mix vegetables, two cups

- Chopped fresh dill, two tbsp.
- Teriyaki sauce, two tbsp.
- Soy sauce, two tbsp.
- Salt to taste
- Black pepper to taste
- Chopped onions, two tbsp.
- Cilantro, as required

Instructions:

1. Cook the udon noodles according to package directions.
2. Meanwhile, in a large wok, stir-fry the vegetables in oil until they get a little soft.
3. Add stir fry sauce and teriyaki sauce.
4. Drain the noodles.
5. Add the noodles and remaining sauces to the wok.
6. Garnish it with cilantro.
7. Your dish is ready to be served.

5.3 Wok Vegan Kimchi Fried Rice

Preparation time: 10 minutes

Cooking Time: 10 minutes

Serving: 4

Ingredients:

- Soy sauce, two tbsp.
- Chopped garlic, two tsp.
- Green onions, three tbsp.
- Kimchi, half cup
- Vegetable oil, two tbsp.
- Salt to taste
- Black pepper to taste
- Cooked rice, two cups
- Mixed nuts, one cup

Instructions:
1. Warm a wok.
2. Add about a tablespoon of oil.
3. Add the diced kimchi and mix attempt until daintily cooked.
4. Add the ginger and garlic to the chicken.
5. Add your rice, somewhat more oil in the event that you need it and mix.
6. Add about a teaspoon of soy sauce to the wok.
7. Add the mixed nuts.
8. Your dish is ready to be served.

5.4 Wok Fried Greens

Preparation time: 25 minutes
Cooking Time: 15 minutes
Serving: 4

Ingredients:

- Asian Sesame oil, two tbsp.
- Chopped garlic, two tsp.
- Green onions, three tbsp.
- Vegetable oil, half cup
- Mix vegetables, two cups
- Chopped fresh dill, two tbsp.
- Soy sauce, two tbsp.
- Salt to taste
- Black pepper to taste
- Flour, one cup
- Egg, one
- Chopped onions, two tbsp.

Instructions:

1. Mix the chopped garlic, green vegetables, sesame oil, soy sauce, salt and pepper together in a bowl.
2. Beat the egg in a separate bowl.

3. Dip the prawns in the egg and then cover with flour.
4. Fry these prawns in a large wok with added oil.
5. Once fried remove from the wok.
6. Add fresh onion and dill on top.
7. Your dish is ready to be served.

5.5 Wok Kale Mushroom and Cashew Stir-Fry

Preparation time: 25 minutes
Cooking Time: 15 minutes
Serving: 4

Ingredients:
- Asian Sesame oil, two tbsp.
- Chopped garlic, two tsp.
- Kale, one cup
- Salt to taste
- Mushroom, one cup
- Cashews, one cup
- Black pepper to taste

Instructions:
1. Heat a large wok.
2. Add the vegetable oil and heat it over high for a few minutes.

3. Add in the garlic and let it brown.
4. Add in the kale, mushrooms and cook it for two minutes.
5. Season generously with kosher salt and pepper.
6. Add in the cashews and fry.
7. Cook for five more minutes.
8. Your dish is ready to be served.

5.6 Wok Seared Vegetables

Preparation time: 25 minutes
Cooking Time: 15 minutes
Serving: 4

Ingredients:
- Oyster sauce, two tbsp.
- Chopped garlic, two tsp.
- Rice wine, two tbsp.
- Mix vegetables, two cups
- Cajun seasoning, two tbsp.
- Vegetable oil, two tbsp.
- Soy sauce, two tbsp.
- Salt to taste
- Black pepper to taste
- Tomatoes, two cups
- Chopped onions, two tbsp.

Instructions:

1. Coat the seasoning on top of the mixed vegetable cubes.
2. Heat a wok.
3. Add the oil and start cooking the mix vegetables until it turns a little crispy.
4. Remove the mixed vegetables and add the onions and garlic into the wok.
5. After cooking the onions, add the vegetables.
6. Add the remaining ingredients and cook for five minutes.
7. Your dish is ready to be served.

5.7 Wok Vegan Japchae

Preparation time: 15 minutes

Cooking Time: 15 minutes

Serving: 4

Ingredients:

- Asian Sesame oil, two tbsp.
- Chopped garlic, two tsp.
- Maggi seasoning, three tbsp.
- Scallions, half cup
- Glass noodles, two cups
- Mix vegetables, two cups
- Vegetable oil, two tbsp.

- Soy sauce, two tbsp.
- Salt to taste
- Black pepper to taste
- Bean sprouts, two cups

Instructions:

1. Cook the glass noodles according to the package instructions.
2. Warm a wok over high warmth for a couple of moments.
3. Coat wok with vegetable oil.
4. Add the vegetables and garlic.
5. Mix everything together, add noodles, and delicately blend.
6. Add Maggi Seasoning and rest of the ingredients.
7. Cook for five minutes.
8. Your dish is ready to be served.

5.8 Creamy Coconut Vegetarian Wok

Preparation time: 25 minutes

Cooking Time: 25 minutes

Serving: 4

Ingredients:

- Asian Sesame oil, two tbsp.
- Chopped garlic, two tsp.
- Green onions, three tbsp.
- Bell pepper strips, half cup
- Coconut milk, two cups
- Chopped fresh dill, two tbsp.
- Vegetable oil, two tbsp.
- Soy sauce, two tbsp.
- Salt to taste
- Black pepper to taste
- Carrots, two cups
- Bean sprouts, one cup
- Peas, one cup
- Shredded coconut, as required
- Chopped onions, two tbsp.

Instructions:
1. In a large wok, add the oil and heat it.
2. Add the garlic and cook.
3. Add in the onions and fry it.
4. Add the vegetables and cook for a few minutes.
5. Add the sauces and coconut milk into the wok and bring to boil.
6. Cook for ten minutes.
7. Garnish with shredded coconut and shallots.

8. Your dish is ready to be served.

5.9 Stir-fried Cucumber

Preparation time: 10 minutes
Cooking Time: 5 minutes
Serving: 4

Ingredients:
- Asian Sesame oil, two tbsp.
- Chopped garlic, two tsp.
- Cooking wine, half cup
- Soy sauce, two tbsp.
- Salt to taste
- Black pepper to taste
- Shredded cucumber, two cups

Instructions:
1. Heat a wok on medium flame.
2. Add the oil and garlic.
3. Cook the garlic, once browned, add the cucumber and cooking wine into it.
4. After the cucumber is wilted and half cooked, add the soy sauce, salt, and pepper.
5. Cook for further ten minutes.

6. Your dish is ready to be served.

5.10 Teriyaki Vegetable Stir-Fry

Preparation time: 30 minutes
Cooking Time: 10 minutes
Serving: 4

Ingredients:
- Sesame oil, one tsp.
- Cornstarch, a quarter cup
- Mix vegetables, one pound
- Teriyaki sauce, a quarter cup
- Soy sauce, one tbsp.
- Garlic powder, half tsp.
- White pepper, a quarter tsp.
- Shaoxing wine, two tbsp.
- Dried chili pepper, six
- Vegetable stock, a quarter cup
- Sugar, two tbsp.
- Star anise, two
- Tangerine peel, two

Instructions:

1. Mix the vegetables in the sesame oil, white pepper, garlic powder, salt, and Shaoxing wine in a wok.
2. Dredge the vegetable pieces in cornstarch and fry until golden.
3. Heat a wok over medium heat and add a tablespoon of oil.
4. Add the dried chili peppers, tangerine peel, and star anise, and toast for about twenty seconds, being careful not to burn the aromatics.
5. Add the teriyaki sauce, vegetable stock, vinegar, sugar, and soy sauce.
6. Bring the sauce to a simmer and gradually add the cornstarch slurry, stirring constantly.
7. Mix all the things together.
8. Your dish is ready to be served.

5.11 Carrot Stir-Fry

Preparation time: 10 minutes

Cooking Time: 5 minutes

Serving: 4

Ingredients:

- Asian Sesame oil, two tbsp.
- Chopped garlic, two tsp.
- Cooking wine, half cup
- Soy sauce, two tbsp.
- Salt to taste
- Black pepper to taste
- Shredded carrots, two cups

Instructions:
1. Heat a wok on medium flame.
2. Add the oil and garlic.
3. Cook the garlic, once browned add the carrots and cooking wine into it.
4. After the carrot is wilted and half cooked, add the soy sauce, salt, and pepper.
5. Cook for further ten minutes.
6. Your dish is ready to be served.

5.12 Vegan Stir Fry with Tempeh and Rice

Preparation time: 10 minutes

Cooking Time: 10 minutes

Serving: 4

Ingredients:
- Soy sauce, two tbsp.
- Chopped garlic, two tsp.

- Green onions, three tbsp.
- Mixed vegetables, two cup
- Vegetable oil, two tbsp.
- Salt to taste
- Black pepper to taste
- Cooked rice, two cups
- Tempeh one cup
- Mixed nuts, one cup

Instructions:
1. Warm a wok.
2. Add about a tablespoon of oil.
3. Add the diced or cut tempeh and mix attempt until daintily cooked.
4. Add the vegetables and cook.
5. Add the ginger and garlic to the wok.
6. Add your rice, somewhat more oil in the event that you need it and mix.
7. Add about a teaspoon of soy sauce to the wok.
8. Add the mixed nuts.
9. Your dish is ready to be served.

5.13 Sesame Ginger and Tofu Stir-Fry

Preparation time: 25 minutes
Cooking Time: 15 minutes

Serving: 4

Ingredients:

- Asian Sesame oil, two tbsp.
- Chopped garlic, two tsp.
- Tofu, one cup
- Salt to taste
- Ginger, half cup
- Sesame seeds, one cup
- Black pepper to taste

Instructions:

1. Heat a large wok.
2. Add the vegetable oil and heat it over high for a few minutes.
3. Add in the garlic and let it brown.
4. Add in the ginger, tofu and cook it for two minutes.
5. Season generously with kosher salt and pepper.
6. Add in the sesame seeds and fry.
7. Cook for five more minutes.
8. Your dish is ready to be served.

5.14 Pumpkin Stir-Fry

Preparation time: 25 minutes

Cooking Time: 15 minutes

Serving: 4

Ingredients:

- Asian Sesame oil, two tbsp.
- Chopped garlic, two tsp.
- Pumpkin, one cup
- Salt to taste
- Mix vegetables, one cup
- Mixed nuts, one cup
- Black pepper to taste

Instructions:

1. Heat a large wok.
2. Add the vegetable oil and heat it over high for a few minutes.
3. Add in the garlic and let it brown.
4. Add in the pumpkin, vegetables and cook it for two minutes.
5. Season generously with kosher salt and pepper.
6. Add in the nuts and fry.
7. Cook for five more minutes.
8. Your dish is ready to be served.

5.15 Wok Vegetable Chowmein

Preparation time: 25 minutes
Cooking Time: 15 minutes
Serving: 4

Ingredients:
- Chopped garlic, two tsp.
- Green onions, three tbsp.
- Bell pepper strips, half cup
- Chow mein noodles, two cups
- Chopped ginger, two tbsp.
- Vegetable oil, two tbsp.
- Soy sauce, two tbsp.
- Salt to taste
- Black pepper to taste
- Mix vegetables, two cups

Instructions:
1. Cook the chowmein noodles as per the course.
2. Channel the noodles whenever they are cooked.
3. Warm the wok over high warmth.
4. In a little bowl, whisk together the wet fixings.
5. Add oil, once hot, add the garlic, carrots, and ginger.

6. Add the remainder of the vegetables and cook them until they are done.
7. Add the cooked noodles and sauce.
8. Mix to consolidate and cook until the sauce has thickened.
9. Add the salt and pepper to the wok.
10. Your dish is fit to be served.

Conclusion

Stir-fry is a method of brisk cooking nourishments with a modest quantity of oil over a high flame. This brilliant cooking strategy from the East adds the flavor, and supplements a dish with aroma. Since cooking goes so rapidly, the primary concern to remember when using stir-frying method is to have every one of your fixings arranged in an order and close nearby before you start cooking.

The Wok is an amazing utensil that has been used for many years in different cuisines around the world. Various cooking methods are deeply influenced by wok cooking. In this book, we discussed the different recipes that originated from a variety of cuisines that has been using a wok since traditional times. Using a wok has been considered very easy and helpful in preparing large batches of food in a short time frame.

We discussed 77 different recipes comprising of breakfast, lunch, dinner, snack, and vegetarian recipes. You can easily make all these recipes at home without any problem with the detailed ingredient list and easy to follow instructions. So, now you can cook easily like a professional using a wok of your own.

Printed in Great Britain
by Amazon